DATE DUE

MAR 4 '70		
MAR 30 '70	MAY 1 2 1993	
APR 6 '70	APR 2 2 1993	
JUN 4 '70		
NOV 2 '70		
APR 26 '71		
DEC 2 '71		
SEP 25 '73		
DEC 19 '73		
JAN 7 '74		
MAY 28 '74		
OCT 2 8 1975		

CANADA

Canada's mountains, forests, and water make superb scenery, as in this view of the Bow River Valley, in Banff National Park, Alberta. The Fairholme Range is in the background. (PHOTO BY LUNNEY, NATIONAL FILM BOARD)

CANADA

by Charles Lineaweaver

Illustrated with photographs

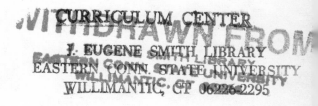

FRANKLIN WATTS, INC.
575 Lexington Avenue • New York, N.Y. 10022

1/70
Library of Congress Catalog Card Number: 67-17788
© Copyright 1967 by Franklin Watts, Inc.
Printed in the United States of America

3 4 5

Contents

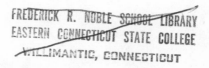

CANADA

In almost every part of Canada there is water in abundance. Scene near Whitefish Falls, Ontario, in the Canadian Shield country. (NATIONAL FILM BOARD)

An Enormous Land – Not Enough People

Canada is the second largest country in the world. Only Russia is bigger. Canada stretches more than four thousand miles from the Atlantic Ocean to the Pacific. From its common border with the United States on the south it pushes three thousand miles north into the polar ice cap of the Arctic Ocean.

The Canadian land has great variety. It has deep forests and vast prairies, tall mountains and flat, frozen arctic areas. And most of all, it has water. Canada is a land of rushing streams, mighty rivers, and shining lakes — thousands of lakes, large and small, scattered thickly over the surface of the earth. Canada has more than one-third of the world's supply of fresh water. With its borders on three oceans and with its thousands of islands offshore, it also has one of the longest seacoasts of any country in the world.

1

About twenty million people live in Canada. One reason there are not more is that the country has three huge areas of land that are half barren. Few plants can grow in some of these places. One of the half-barren areas is the Arctic, made up of one million square miles too cold for any trees to grow there. Another of these areas is the great mountain-range section of the west, where about one hundred mountains are ten thousand feet high or more. Most plants can grow only on their lower slopes. The third area is the so-called Canadian Shield — nearly two million square miles of land surrounding Hudson Bay and stretching from the Atlantic Ocean to the Arctic Ocean. Many thousands of years ago, the glaciers of the Ice Age scraped nearly all the soil away from parts of this section. Remaining is a low plateau, or upland, of age-old rock, rounded hills, shallow lakes, and swamps, none of which is good for farming. Still, with all the country's water and with half a million square miles of land suitable for cultivation, Canada could support a larger population than it has.

The half-barren areas take up nearly three-quarters of the country. Because these areas are not very good living places, most Canadians have their homes in a narrow belt of land that stretches the length of the United States border. There are no major cities more than two hundred miles north of this border, although some important mining towns and some seaports lie farther away. Within this narrow populated belt of land there are widely varied places, from huge cities to endless prairies, from small, neat farms to enormous cattle ranches, from the French villages dotting the shores of

A modern Canadian farm in southern Ontario. (PHOTO BY HUFFMAN, FROM CUSHING)

In the prairie provinces, huge grain fields stretch away toward the horizon. (MANITOBA DEPT. OF INDUSTRY & COMMERCE PHOTO)

the St. Lawrence River in the province of Quebec to the tiny towns huddled around grain elevators along the railroad lines of the western plains.

Down East are the four Atlantic provinces: Newfoundland, Prince Edward Island, New Brunswick, and Nova Scotia. The people of these provinces earn their living mainly at fishing, working with forest products, manufacturing, farming, and mining.

Next westward from the Atlantic provinces lie Quebec and Ontario. Here are the fertile St. Lawrence River lowlands. In their moderate climate, fruits, vegetables, and tobacco grow well. Here in the lowlands most of Canada's manufacturing is done, and here are the two largest cities, Montreal and Toronto. Both Quebec and Ontario extend far to the north into the rich mining country of the Canadian Shield. These two provinces are Canada's greatest producers of minerals.

Between Ontario and the Rocky Mountains lie the great inland plains of Manitoba, Saskatchewan, and Alberta. Because of its deep clay soil, this flat, treeless prairie land is one of the world's greatest grain-growing areas.

3

On Canada's west coast, forested mountains meet the ocean. (BRITISH COLUMBIA GOVT. PHOTO)

Finally, there is the province of British Columbia, lying along the Pacific Ocean. The large forests growing on the flanks of its great mountains provide almost limitless timber. In the fertile river valleys of the southern part of the province magnificent fruits and vegetables are produced. On the coast and in the big rivers enough fish are caught to earn nearly one-third of Canada's total income from sea fish.

Of Canada's twenty million people, more than forty per cent are of British descent, and about thirty per cent are of French descent. The French live mainly in the province of Quebec. Germans are Canada's third largest national group, followed by Ukrainians, Italians, Dutch, Scandinavians, and Poles. Since World War II, however, immigrants have come from more than forty countries.

4

Now Canada has every bit as much variety in its people as in its geography. There are newspapers published in more than forty languages. There is broadcasting in many tongues, and worshiping in many religions. Each group of immigrants has kept the best part of its own customs and ways of doing things. And each group has kept somewhat apart from the others, in its own place, so that it still has something of its own particular national quality.

A century ago, when Canada became a dominion, two official national languages were approved: French and English. The French-speaking and English-speaking groups each have their own ways of living and thinking. They are quite different. Although the two groups are officially recognized as equal, there are misunderstandings and jealousies between them. Recently this situation has led to a new kind of national feeling in the province of Quebec. There the French Canadians are determined to be complete masters of their own future. Some of the groups with the strongest feeling have even wanted to set up a separate French nation. Up to now, cooler and more thoughtful people have been against this, and it seems unlikely that the separate-nation idea will be carried out.

Canadians are generally said to be much like the people of the United States. In many ways they are. But there are important differences. One is that Canada has two official languages and two major ways of living — French and English. Another is that most of the people live very close to nature. Even in a great city like Montreal, the wilderness is only a short distance from a Canadian's front door. The Canadian people are always aware of the great empty spaces so near at hand. As their country grows they see the opportunity and the challenge of their wilderness areas.

From Innuit to Independence

In Canada before the white men there were the Indians and the Eskimos, who called themselves Innuit, "the People." No one knows how long they had been in the land before the Europeans discovered it, but certainly these earlier people had been there for three or four thousand years.

As long ago as a thousand years the Vikings had colonies in Newfoundland. The remains of these colonies have been discovered and are now being unearthed. Were the Vikings the first Europeans to reach America? There is good reason to believe not. Five hundred years before even the Vikings found this country that they called Vinland, Irish monks may have come across the Atlantic as Christian missionaries to this new and savage world. The earliest French settlers in Nova Scotia heard the Indians tell tales of white men in white robes from across the sea. Without written history such things are hard to prove. But it is strange that certain of the Indian words, as well as certain words of the eastern Eskimos, are much like the Celtic language that was in use in Ireland at that early time. They are, however.

For some five centuries after the Vikings left, the New World was forgotten by Europe. Not until a search for a westerly passage to the riches of the Orient became important did the Europeans return. In 1492, Columbus sailed southwest to the Caribbean islands and thought he had found the Indies. A few years later, John Cabot, exploring for England, tried to find a northwest passage to the Orient. Instead, he found Newfoundland and the continent of North America.

After the Spanish and English voyages the interest of France was aroused. In 1534, Jacques Cartier arrived to plant a cross on the mainland at what is now the Gaspé Peninsula in the province of Quebec and to claim the land for France. The next year he found the St. Lawrence River. But his hopeful sail upriver to the westward, deep into the continent, was ended when he came to the rapids at the site of the present city of Montreal. They could not be passed by ships.

Sebastian Cabot, son of John Cabot, accompanied his father and two brothers on voyages to the New World in 1497 and 1499. In this engraving from a picture by E. Bayard, Sebastian is shown taking leave of Labrador. (PHOTO BY CHARLES PHELPS CUSHING)

Portrait of Jacques Cartier, French discoverer and explorer of the St. Lawrence River. (PHOTO BY CHARLES PHELPS CUSHING)

Years later the true founder of New France, Samuel de Champlain, was sent by his country to find the westward passage that men were sure was there. In 1604, Champlain made the first permanent settlement north of Florida. It was at Port Royal in Nova Scotia. Four years later he founded the village of Quebec at a towering rock overlooking the St. Lawrence River. There the city has remained, standing today as the spectacular capital of its province.

As the years passed, men began to realize that Canada did not have a westward passage for ships. They began to see, however, that this new land could be important for itself — a vast country of riches waiting to be found and made use of. Restless and daring, Champlain spent years in the lonely forests, venturing on lakes and rivers and Indian trails. A map of eastern Canada began to take shape.

View of Quebec, one of the oldest cities in North America. Kent Gate, in the foreground, is one of three gates remaining in the wall that once enclosed the city. (NATIONAL FILM BOARD)

An old print of a band of early French trappers making their way up-river to hunt for furs. (PHOTO BY CHARLES PHELPS CUSHING)

Then the beaver hat became fashionable in Europe and the demand for beaver skins began. As more and more skins were needed, the French pushed ever farther westward to trade with the Indians. Even at a time when the British colonists to the south had not moved more than a few miles from the eastern seaboard, the French had come out onto Lake Superior, halfway across the continent.

Hearing stories of the Mississippi, Father Marquette and his companion, Louis Jolliet, explored in 1673 to see if the great river might be a passage to the west. They went downriver as far as present-day Arkansas before they gave up their search. Their unsuccessful trip inspired another explorer, the Sieur de La Salle, to voyage to the mouth of the Mississippi and claim for France an enormous territory important to the ever greater hunt for fur. Because of her claim to this territory, France was able to hem in the English colonies by a thin line of forts and trading posts that dotted the wilderness from Quebec to New Orleans.

9

Portrait of chief Joseph Brant, who was one of the leaders of the Iroquois Indians in the eighteenth century. Brantford, Ontario, named for him, is still the headquarters of the united Iroquois tribes of the Six Nations. (PHOTO BY CHARLES PHELPS CUSHING)

There was one hitch, however. The French had made lasting enemies of the Iroquois Indians by taking sides against them with their enemies, the Hurons. Because the Iroquois were able to control long stretches of the normal fur routes from the west to Quebec and Montreal, a different way to get furs out of Canada was needed. This way led through Hudson Bay. France was not interested in this route. England was. So the Hudson's Bay Company was formed. In 1670 it was chartered by the English to trade into areas that could be reached by sea, through Hudson Bay. Today this company remains the oldest in North America. Because of its early interests, the first conflicts between the French and the English in Canada began. The English laid claim to all the land north and west of the French settlements and forts. For many years there were frontier raids and battles, with some Indian tribes supporting one side, some the other. And so the struggles for trade continued until the decisive year of 1759.

The Evangeline statue and shrine at Grand Pré, Nova Scotia, commemorate the exiling of the French in 1755. (PHOTO BY CHARLES PHELPS CUSHING)

In preparing for the contest that could not be avoided, both France and England tried to build new and stronger defenses. The English already held part of Nova Scotia. They believed that the French inhabitants there might not be loyal in the forthcoming war, since these inhabitants refused to take an oath of allegiance to the British Crown. So the English decided to expel the French from Acadia, as the area was then called. Ships were made ready and, in the summer of 1755, hundreds of miserable people were torn from their homes. Their property was destroyed and their families were divided. Some were sent to Europe, while others were scattered through the thirteen colonies to the south to make their way as best they could. This sad event in Canada's history is the subject of the famous poem "Evangeline," by Henry Wadsworth Longfellow. In the southern part of the United States, especially in Louisiana, the word "Acadian" gradually became the term "Cajun," which is still applied to American southerners of French descent.

11

The deciding battle of the long struggle came four years after the driving out of the Acadians. The fortress city of Quebec, under the command of the French Marquis de Montcalm, fell to the British under Major General James Wolfe. In the fierce fighting outside the city walls, on the Plains of Abraham, both commanding officers were killed. When the smoke of battle had cleared, New France had fallen. The British had gained Canada.

BRITISH NORTH AMERICA

When the American Revolution began, many of the rebels in the thirteen colonies hoped that the French would join in the overthrow of British rule. This was not to be, thanks partly to the generosity that the British had shown in the so-called Quebec Act. Under this act the conquered French in Canada were officially allowed to keep their language, their Roman Catholic religion, and their own civil law and system of landholding.

In addition, at the time of the Revolution, some forty thousand people who wished to remain loyal to the British Crown arrived in

An old engraving of the death of General Wolfe, who captured Quebec, but lost his life in the battle. His last words are said to have been, "Now I die contented." (PHOTO BY CHARLES PHELPS CUSHING)

Canada from the English colonies to the south. These people, called United Empire Loyalists, strengthened Canada's ties to Great Britain.

For a century, Canada was a British colony, though all during this time there was a slow movement toward self-government. More and more immigrants came, as Europeans sought free land in the New World. The explorers of the vast lands to the west were followed by settlers who carved farmlands and villages out of the wilderness. Logging in Quebec and along the Atlantic Coast grew in importance. The shipbuilding industry began to thrive, and growing businesses started to edge out the fur trade in importance.

In the first half of the nineteenth century there was overcrowding and unemployment in the British Isles, and the terrible Potato Famine in Ireland. With bigger and bigger ships crossing the Atlantic, more than eight hundred thousand immigrants arrived in Canada, and its population tripled. As the country grew, the people in the underdeveloped West had almost no communication with the people in the settled East. The interests of neighbors across the Canadian-United States border were often closer than those of Canadians who had thousands of miles of land between them in their own country. There was a need to link the various parts of Canada together in order to prevent the possible union of some sections with neighboring parts of the United States.

When, in 1864, a meeting was held on Prince Edward Island to discuss a Maritime Federation, Upper and Lower Canada (now Ontario and Quebec) were invited to give their opinions on joining together all the British colonies in North America. Out of this meeting and many later conferences came the British North America Act, creating a union of the colonies, which up to that time had been separate. A new nation, Canada, was born as a dominion of Great Britain. The year was 1867; the actual day was July 1. That day is now nationally celebrated as Dominion Day.

Canada's first prime minister, and one of her greatest, was Sir John A. Macdonald. He encouraged the settlement of the West and the building of a transcontinental railroad. He realized how important transportation was to Canada; the narrow belt of populated land could not possibly be held together without rapid communication. From Macdonald's time on, the history of the country has been enormously influenced by the railways. Present-day Canada has more miles of railroad per person than any other country has.

It was due to the promise of a coast-to-coast railroad that the province of British Columbia came into the federation and gave the country its spread from the Atlantic to the Pacific. With the completion of the Canadian Pacific Railway in 1885, the face of the West was changed forever. In the next twenty-five years, two million immigrants, largely from Central Europe, arrived. Most of them settled on the prairies. That former country of roving Indians and buffalo herds became a land of grain farmers as the plains were slowly turned into wheat fields. Manitoba had become a province in 1870, and in 1905 she was joined by Saskatchewan and Alberta. Not until 1949, when Newfoundland became the tenth province, could Canada really claim that her dominion spread from sea to sea, however. *A Mari Usque Ad Mare* is her Latin motto; it means "From Sea to Sea." (Both the word "dominion" and the words of the motto can be found in the Bible. In the Book of Zechariah is the phrase, "and his dominion shall be from sea to sea.")

With Canada leading the way, the British Empire became the British Commonwealth, and in 1926 its nations were declared to be "equal in status, in no way subordinate one to another in any aspect of their domestic or external affairs." Accordingly, Canada today is a wholly independent country, making her own laws, con-

14

ducting her own foreign affairs, maintaining her own armed forces, her own diplomatic service, and her own system of money.

Canada is a union, or federation, of provinces, each with a great deal of power for self-government. The federal government in Ottawa, the capital, is modeled on the British government, with a Parliament as its lawmaking body. There are two houses in Parliament: the Senate and the House of Commons. The members of the Senate are *appointed* on a regional basis by the Governor-General on the recommendation of the Prime Minister. The members of the House of Commons are *elected* directly by the people.

After an election, the government is formed by the party having the largest number of members in the House of Commons. The leader of this party becomes the Prime Minister. He does not hold office for a definite term, but only for as long as his party can control the majority of votes in the House of Commons on important matters.

Although the British Sovereign is the nominal head of state and

An air view of a section of Ottawa, Canada's capital. In the center are the Parliament Buildings, overlooking the Ottawa River, with the city of Hull in the background. (PHOTOGRAPHIC SURVEY CORP. PHOTO)

is represented by an appointed Governor-General, it is the Prime Minister, his Cabinet, and the members of the House of Commons who are responsible for making laws and running the various departments and agencies of the government. If the majority party in Commons loses control of the votes, the government may be toppled at any time, and new elections will then be called. But a general election *must* be held after one party has been in power for five years. This is to make sure that the voters of the country are truly being represented by the political party they themselves prefer.

Each of the ten provinces has its own government, which in form is much like the elected government in Ottawa. Under the British North America Act the provinces were granted powers in matters of purely local concern, such as civil rights, health, education, property laws, and the management of Crown or public lands. In Quebec both French and English remain official and commonly used languages. Not only may either be used in provincial affairs but also either may be used in the federal Parliament and in any federal court in the country. In the remaining provinces, English is the accepted language.

Lying north of the provinces and making up the rest of Canada are the Yukon Territory and the Northwest Territories. Each has one elected member in the government at Ottawa.

Locally the Yukon Territory is governed by an appointed resident commissioner and a legislative council of seven members chosen by the people in local elections. The capital is Whitehorse.

The Northwest Territories are governed from Yellowknife by an appointed commissioner and a council of nine members, four of whom are elected and five appointed. Until the population of the North greatly increases, it is likely that the Northwest Territories will remain under the federal Department of Northern Affairs, which is also responsible for the Eskimos and the resources of this vast, generally empty area.

The Atlantic Provinces — Forests, Farms, and Fish

While they are small in size compared to the rest of the country, the four Atlantic provinces are far from alike. What they do have in common are the ocean, the swirling fogs and slashing storms, and more important, the fisheries.

Prince Edward Island, Canada's littlest province, is a low, fertile land, more than four-fifths of which is farming country.

Farms and farming villages dot the fertile countryside of Prince Edward Island. The island is famous for its dairy products and potatoes. (CANADIAN GOVT. TRAVEL BUREAU PHOTO)

In Nova Scotia the waves break white along the rocky promontories, and deep little coves provide safe harbor. Air view of the coast. (NOVA SCOTIA INFORMATION SERVICE PHOTO)

Eighty per cent of New Brunswick, its neighbor across the narrow Northumberland Strait, is covered with forests, which spread across its hills and low mountains.

Nova Scotia, a peninsula jutting into the Atlantic, has a long, rugged coast carved out by the sea into many fine harbors. Its gentle inland country is a patchwork of farms and apple orchards.

Because of its rocky soil, Newfoundland has almost no farming. Its six-thousand-mile-long, rockbound seacoast is dotted with fishing villages, called outports, and its uninhabited inland is a wilderness of lakes, forests, and muskeg — boggy country. Besides the island of that name, the province of Newfoundland also includes the rugged mainland region of Labrador, stretching north to the Arctic.

Newfoundland and Nova Scotia, particularly, draw much of their livelihood from the sea. Today's fishing industry seems far removed from the past time of iron men and wooden ships. Now great modern trawlers have replaced the famous schooners known as bankers, which once swarmed over the Grand Banks of Newfoundland, fishing for cod. Today, while some of the catch is still salted and dried as it used to be, more of it is canned or frozen in newly built plants. Preserved in this way, it is shipped to all parts

Fishermen at work on a Nova Scotia trawler clean their catch. (NOVA SCOTIA INFORMATION TRAVEL BUREAU PHOTO)

Fishing boats moored at a typical outpost in Newfoundland. (CANADIAN GOVT. TRAVEL BUREAU PHOTO)

of the world. New ways are being tried out to improve the size of the catch, which, besides cod, includes haddock, halibut, herring, and lobsters. In one experiment, the "Peeping Tom," divers working underwater are learning why some fish escape from nets and traps. From the knowledge so gained, better designs for nets may come, and new and better fishing grounds may be found.

The idea for frozen foods originated in Labrador, the mainland part of the province of Newfoundland. Clarence Birdseye, a citizen of the United States, was engaged in fur trading in Labrador before World War I. In the arctic winter he noticed that the fish he caught froze almost instantly. But when they were later thawed out and cooked they tasted as if they had been freshly caught. He had the same experience with caribou meat, with ducks and geese, and later with vegetables. Upon returning home, he spent years in experimenting, and finally found a method of quick-freezing that could be used commercially. Nowadays, frozen foods rank with fresh foods in popularity, and delicious meats and vegetables of all kinds may be bought throughout the year.

In spite of its fishing, Newfoundland's major industry is manufacturing, especially wood pulp and paper products. The largest paper mill in the world is at Corner Brook, in Newfoundland. The two Atlantic provinces of Newfoundland and New Brunswick contribute much to making the manufacture of pulp and paper one of Canada's leading industries. The country supplies more than half the newsprint needs of the world.

Corner Brook, Newfoundland, is famous for its flourishing pulpwood industry. (CANADIAN GOVT. TRAVEL BUREAU PHOTO)

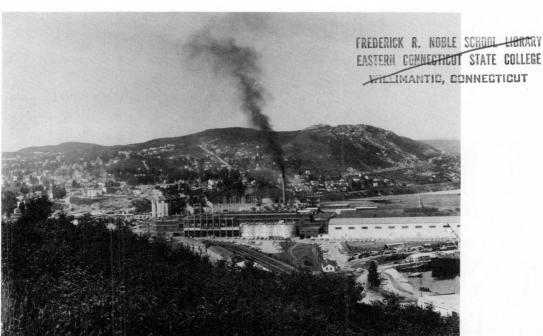

Witless Bay, one of Newfoundland's many small natural harbors, is lined with "fish flakes" — racks where fish are spread to dry. (CANADIAN GOVT. TRAVEL BUREAU PHOTO)

Iron ore from Newfoundland and coal from Nova Scotia have combined to make a steel industry important to Nova Scotia. Copper, lead, and zinc are mined and smelted in Newfoundland. But the color of Newfoundland comes from the seafaring life on the North Atlantic, and many of the place-names show it. That this is a hard life is shown by such names as Misery Point, Breakheart Point, Mistaken Point, and Confusion Bay. A seafaring life is a lonely one, with the sight of home a welcome one. There is a Safe Harbor. There are Comfort Cove and Sweet Bay. Here, too, as in every life where men face the unknown or are beset by sudden danger, is humor. There is a Blow Me Down, a Come By Chance, and a Jerry's Nose. These are the places that dot the coast — the places from which, for centuries, men have gone out to sea in their boats.

Newfoundland is an island of many "firsts" that have helped pave the way for the development of worldwide communications. In 1866 the first transatlantic cable was laid between Newfoundland's village of Heart's Content and Ireland. Thirty-five years later, Guglielmo Marconi received the first transatlantic wireless message from England at Signal Hill near St. John's, the capital of New-foundland. In 1919, two fliers, John William Alcock and Arthur Whitten Brown, made the first nonstop transatlantic airplane flight, from Newfoundland to Ireland, and so foreshadowed our Air Age in which giant jetliners crisscross the globe twenty-four hours a day. Now Newfoundland's airports of Gander and Goose Bay are important stops for many transatlantic planes.

Just as there is a contrast in the geography of the Atlantic provinces, so there is also a contrast in the people. In Halifax, the capital of Nova Scotia, live thousands of Negroes, the descendants of runaway slaves from farther south. There are Germans and Dutch on the coast. And on Cape Breton Island, in the northeastern part of the province, there are so many Scots that each summer there is a Gaelic Mod. This is a festival of Scottish songs and dances. Nova Scotia also boasts a Gaelic college and newspaper. Gaelic is the traditional language of the Scottish Highlanders.

A bagpiper plays for kilted dancers at the annual Gaelic Mod on Cape Breton Island. (NOVA SCOTIA INFORMATION SERVICE PHOTO)

On the other hand, New Brunswick is half French, and many of the villages, with their twin-towered Catholic churches, look as if they really should belong in neighboring Quebec.

But there is still much of the early Indian in New Brunswick, and while Newfoundland has strange place-names in English, New Brunswick has them in Algonquin. In a famous poem about these names are the lines,

> *Ah, no! in New Brunswick we'll find it,*
> *A sweetly sequestered nook —*
> *Where the slow-gliding Skoodawabskooksis*
> *Unites with the Skoodawabskook!*

One of the dreams of the people of the Atlantic provinces is a direct road straight across the state of Maine. Such a road would bring the big towns and cities of Quebec and Ontario some two hundred miles closer for travelers from the coast. It is believed that each year more than three million vehicles would use such a corridor road to avoid the roundabout all-Canadian route that pushes over the top of Maine and far north into Quebec and New Brunswick. A direct highway would make it easier and less expensive to transport to market the fish, the oysters and lobsters, and the farm and forest products on which the Atlantic area depends so heavily.

Lumber is moved from these snow-covered forests in New Brunswick.
(NEW BRUNSWICK TRAVEL BUREAU PHOTO)

Thetford Mines, in Quebec, is the center of the world's leading asbestos-producing region. (PHOTO BY JARRETT, NATIONAL FILM BOARD)

The St. Lawrence Lowlands – the Cradle of Canada

Much of the country's past lies in the long St. Lawrence River Valley and the Great Lakes region to the west. And much of its future will lie here too. Here are Canada's largest cities — Montreal, in Quebec, and Toronto, in Ontario, as well as the capital, Ottawa.

This area is Canada's industrial heart. Here great factories turn out everything from automobiles to railway locomotives, from steel plates to plastics. In Quebec are two of Canada's greatest hydroelectric plants, which produce electricity from the energy of rapidly running water. They are at Shipshaw, on the Saguenay River, and at Beauharnois, on the St. Lawrence. At these and other hydroelectric plants in the province, power is produced for the pulp and paper mills, for the gigantic aluminum smelters and steel plants. Because of its great power development the province of Quebec has enough varied manufacturing to produce one-third of Canada's

26

goods. Neighboring Ontario is an even heavier industrial area. It produces one-half the country's goods.

Because both Quebec and Ontario stretch up into the Canadian Shield they produce many minerals. Quebec has large iron deposits, besides gold, copper, zinc, silver, and other metals. In the southern part of the province, seventy per cent of the world's asbestos is mined. But Ontario is the leading mining province of Canada. It produces one-quarter of the country's minerals — gold, silver, copper, zinc, and the world's greatest supply of nickel.

Niagara Falls is, of course, one of the best-known tourist attractions in North America. The spectacular drop of the Niagara River for more than three hundred feet creates a roaring cascade that

The American Falls and the Canadian Horseshoe Falls, in the background, drop to the narrow gorge through which the Niagara River rushes on its way to Lake Ontario and the sea. (CANADIAN GOVT. TRAVEL BUREAU PHOTO)

sends mists swirling high into the air above it. The thunder of the waters is always present in the twin cities of Niagara Falls, Ontario, and Niagara Falls, New York. The falls are not just a tourist show, however. They have been a major source of power ever since 1893, when the river was first turned aside for the generating of electricity. This turning aside is something like shutting off a part of the falls, although by terms of a treaty between Canada and the United States both countries are limited in the amount of water they can take.

To produce electricity, water is taken from the river above the falls and is channeled underground through what are called power canals. The water flows into power stations, where it turns giant turbines and so generates electric current. From the power stations the familiar lofty transmission lines fan out across the country to carry the electricity wherever it is needed to light farms and cities and to turn the wheels of industry. The Niagara River is only one of the many sources of hydroelectric power in the St. Lawrence lowlands. Power is abundant, it is close at hand, and it is inexpensive.

The already prosperous lowlands area was recently helped even more by the completion of the St. Lawrence Seaway. It had long been a Canadian dream to deepen the ship canals along the river so that seagoing vessels could sail right into the Great Lakes and the heart of the continent. Formerly, cargoes had to be reloaded at Montreal. Outgoing, the cargoes were transferred from the small lake-going ships to the large freighters that went out across the oceans and around the world. Incoming, the cargoes had to be unloaded and then put aboard the small ships that could navigate the old canal system. Canada spent many years in negotiating with the United States about the Seaway. Only when Canada seemed likely to proceed alone with an all-Canadian canal did the two countries reach agreement to work together. The completed Seaway was opened in 1959 by Queen Elizabeth II, Sovereign of Canada, and President Eisenhower of the United States.

28

The locks of the St. Lawrence Seaway are operated night and day during the ice-free navigation season. The ship in the foreground is in St. Lambert Lock, the first of seven between Montreal and Lake Ontario. Beyond the lock are the lights of Montreal. (ST. LAWRENCE SEAWAY PHOTO)

A tobacco farm in Ontario. After the leaves have been gathered, they are cured in the sheds in the background. (ONTARIO DEPT. OF TOURISM PHOTO)

Today inland ports like Toronto and Hamilton and Port Arthur in Canada, and Cleveland and Chicago and Duluth in the United States have become seaports, for all practical purposes. The Great Lakes are open to all but the largest ocean-going ships, and flags from the nations of the world now flutter across what, a short time ago, were inland harbors. Since the Seaway was built around shallows and rapids, Canada and the United States have developed new power-generating systems to give the area even more electricity and so make sure of more new factories and industrial plants.

Beyond the cities and the humming factory towns of the lowlands lie some of Canada's most fertile farmlands. There are dairy farms, and farms that grow clover, hay, and potatoes. Great quantities of fine tobacco are also grown here. Market gardening is important and so is the growing of fruit, especially apples, peaches, cherries, and grapes for a flourishing wine industry. Ontario's Niagara Peninsula is famous for its orchards. Each spring thousands of people come from both sides of the border to see the miles of blossoming trees.

Separating the provinces of Ontario and Quebec is the Ottawa River. Up the river, one hundred miles from where it flows into the St. Lawrence at Montreal, is Canada's capital, Ottawa. High above the city the beautiful three-hundred-foot-tall Peace Tower rises on Parliament Hill, dwarfing the Parliament buildings that surround

The Peace Tower, framed by an archway, in Ottawa. (ONTARIO DEPT. OF TOURISM PHOTO)

it. Each day, over the sounds of the city, there can be heard the magnificent carillon — fifty-three bells ringing out from the tower in memory of Canada's service in World War I. The largest bell weighs more than eleven tons — the smallest, ten pounds. Their lovely sound carries far across the capital's canals, its river, its shaded drives and, in spring, across a million tulips. These were the gift of the Netherlands, for it was in Ottawa that the Dutch Queen Juliana found refuge during World War II, when her country was overrun by the enemy.

Each day, too, in the summer months, the colorful ceremony of the Changing of the Guard takes place. And for the benefit of visitors in Ottawa, most of whom carry cameras, the Mounties, Canada's Mounted Police, may be seen on Capitol Hill in their traditional red coats, no longer their ordinary working uniform.

Although Canada has been a nation for a century, she did not have an official national flag until 1965. Various flags have flown over her and have been in use — from the St. George's Cross carried by John Cabot, through the flag of France and the Union Jack, to the Red Ensign. This flag, used by the British merchant marine, was allowed on Canadian ships when it was shown with Canada's shield in the fly. Gradually it came to be flown on Canadian buildings abroad, and finally on federal buildings inside the country as well. But with Canada's one-hundredth anniversary coming in 1967, it was finally decided that a true Canadian flag must be designed — a flag not borrowed from the British. Canada's new flag uses the maple leaf, which for more than two hundred and fifty years has been considered a Canadian symbol. The flag is basically red, with a square white center that contains an eleven-pointed red maple leaf. Because this flag does not bring to mind Canada's former ties to any European country, it appears to satisfy most of the people, whatever their national background may be.

32

Since 1965, the Canadian national flag has been a red maple leaf on a field of white, flanked by two red rectangles.

Toronto, on the shores of Lake Ontario, is Ontario's largest city and the capital of the province. It is the ever growing commercial center of the country and is becoming more and more aware of the rest of the world as its industry has attracted great numbers of foreign-born immigrants since World War II.

Toronto is a great sports town, with football and baseball teams, and a famous National League hockey team.

Hockey is Canada's top sport and is played from coast to coast. Children learn to skate almost as soon as they can walk. Almost every town and village floods an outdoor area to provide a skating rink. And even some of the smaller towns have their own arenas and belong to one of the countless hockey leagues that operate from Newfoundland to British Columbia. Many Canadian boys dream of playing in the "big league," either for the Toronto Maple Leafs or for Montreal's Canadiens, the "Flying Frenchmen."

A huge lighted cross on Mount Royal in Montreal is a reminder of the wooden one placed there more than three centuries ago by French explorers.

Bigger and older than Toronto is Montreal, in the province of Quebec. It is the second-largest French-speaking city in the world, as well as the greatest inland port. Above the center of the sprawling city looms Mount Royal, a beautiful park that allows outdoor sports in the heart of town. A huge lighted cross on the mountaintop recalls the wooden one set up more than three centuries ago by the Sieur de Maisonneuve, the founder of the little mission that grew into this great metropolis.

Like all major seaports, Montreal is colorful, exciting, and worldly because of the ships coming and going, with their men from many lands. It is a city of contrasts, with narrow cobblestone-paved streets and old churches beside towering office buildings and wide boulevards. Three-quarters of Montreal's two million or so

34

A portion of Montreal's harbor, with the city beyond. (NATIONAL FILM BOARD)

inhabitants are French-speaking, and if there is any true mixing of Canada's two largest national groups, Montreal is the center of it. In Montreal, as elsewhere in the province of Quebec, all elementary and secondary schools teach both the French and English languages.

Just outside the city is the Mohawk Indian reservation of Caughnawaga. Its men are famous high-steel-construction workers and are called all over the continent to help in the building of bridges and high-rise steel frames. Apparently, even at great heights, they are completely unaffected by dizziness. The presence of these Indians at Caughnawaga can be said to remind Montrealers of the past, when the little fortified mission called Ville-Marie de Montréal was under almost constant attack from the Iroquois Nation and especially from the ancestors of these same now friendly Mohawks.

Huge combines harvest grain on the flat prairie land of Saskatchewan.
(SASKATCHEWAN GOVT. PHOTO)

The Prairie Provinces – Canada's Breadbasket

The plains area lies from Ontario west to the Rocky Mountains. It is mostly a flat, treeless expanse that seems to stretch on forever. This is the land of wheat, of oats, of barley, and of cattle raising. The three prairie provinces, Manitoba, Saskatchewan, and Alberta, stretch far north, however. Beyond the farmlands there are mining and lumbering, as well as commercial fishing in the numerous large lakes.

Though today the plains have many industries, Canada's West was built on wheat. One reason for this was that here was developed a quick-ripening hard wheat that met the world's demand for better flour. There were other reasons, too. There was the im-

Along the railroads of the prairie provinces, tall grain elevators rise.
(MANITOBA DEPT. OF INDUSTRY & COMMERCE PHOTO)

proved farm machinery — the giant combines that cut, thresh, and load in one continuous operation. There was the building of the railways and the development of the whalebacks — Great Lakes freighters especially designed for carrying grain cargoes. And there was the building of the little storage elevators that dot the landscape along the railroads, and of the huge elevators at lake and ocean ports, with their efficient machinery for loading and unloading. All these things added up to make the most expert handling of grain shipments the world had ever seen. By the time of World War I, Canada had become the Number One wheat-exporting country. Because of the immense grain traffic, Winnipeg, the capi-

38

tal of Manitoba, grew into a great city. All Canada's transcontinental railway lines pass through it. In addition to having the continent's greatest wheat market, it has tremendous stockyards and meat-packing plants, for the plains are beef country, too.

Starting as a fur-trading post, Winnipeg became the home of the first white settlers on the plains in 1812. In that year the Hudson's Bay Company, seeing the possibilities of the fertile Red River Valley, brought a group of Scottish settlers to what is now Winnipeg. Years of cruel hardship followed for the colony, but slowly it grew, and gradually more settlers arrived. In 1873 the settlement received the name "Winnipeg" and was incorporated as a city.

While ordinarily we do not think of the central prairies as lying anywhere near salt water, the province of Manitoba has a long coastline. Four hundred miles of it lie along Hudson Bay. During the short shipping season of that far-north region, more than twenty

Main Street, Winnipeg, 1870, looking north. From a watercolor by E. J. Hutchins. (PUBLIC ARCHIVES OF CANADA)

During the summer months, Churchill, Manitoba, on Hudson Bay, is an important grain-loading port. (MANITOBA DEPT. OF INDUSTRY & COMMERCE PHOTO)

million bushels of wheat are loaded aboard ocean-going ships. The port is Churchill, lying deep in the Canadian Shield. Enormous Hudson Bay is almost an inland sea. Always cold, mostly icebound, and plunging deep into the heart of the country, the bay causes the severity of the winter and the coolness of the summer over much of Canada.

West of Manitoba is Saskatchewan with its capital of Regina. Here one of the most interesting attractions is the Royal Canadian Mounted Police Museum. In 1883 the city became the western headquarters for this famous police force, which was then known as the North West Mounted Police. Ten years earlier the force had been organized by the government, which believed that a police force would do more to prevent lawlessness than a military garrison

The Royal Canadian Mounted Police Museum in Regina, Saskatchewan, displays a variety of fascinating objects, among them an old cannon and shells, a still, and a Japanese balloon. (SASKATCHEWAN GOVT. PHOTO)

would. One particular trouble was the smuggling of whisky to the Indians. This was mostly the work of United States citizens, who had even set up a base in Canada over which flew the Stars and Stripes. With good reason, the base was called Fort Whoop-up. The red-coated Mounties broke up the whisky trade. At the same time they won the respect of the Indians and helped them settle on reservations and adjust from their former life of wandering. Because of the Mounties and the faith the Indians had in their word, the Canadian West was opened to settlement without the fierce and tragic warring that occurred in the United States. The Mounties' word was their bond, and because the Indians knew it they regarded the police as their friends.

With the settlement of the West, the name and duties of the

police were changed. Today, as the Royal Canadian Mounted Police, the force is responsible for enforcing federal law throughout the dominion. This modern force of more than six thousand men is trained in the latest crime-detection methods at a police college. The force has aviation and marine sections, scientific laboratories, and electronic equipment. While it is very different from the first small group that tracked through the wilds with horses, dogsleds, and canoes, it is the same in one way. It always aims to live up to its motto, *Maintiens le Droit* — Uphold the Right.

A Royal Canadian Mounted Police trumpeter stands by a fountain in the Legislative Grounds at Regina, Saskatchewan. (SASKATCHEWAN GOVT. PHOTO)

The Peace River Valley in Alberta is far north, but its fertile land and long summer days make it a great farming area. (ALBERTA GOVT. PHOTO)

Far to the west of Hudson Bay, and the Canadian Shield that surrounds it, lies the valley of the Peace River, in Alberta. In spite of its location far north, this valley is Canada's last great farming frontier. The growing season is short — not more than three months — but with twenty hours of sunlight in the long days of the northern summer, crops flourish and livestock thrives. Over one hundred thousand people live in this fertile area, remote though it is from the big towns and the industry of the south.

Because the northern parts of the prairie provinces thrust into the Canadian Shield, all three are producers of minerals. Oil has been drilled here for more than fifty years. But it was the discovery in 1947 of the Leduc field near Edmonton, Alberta's capital, that brought about a major change in the economic life of the area. Oil is found in all three of the prairie provinces; it has replaced gold as Canada's most important mineral product. In Edmonton and in Calgary, Alberta's second-largest city, live thousands of Americans

43

who came north to work in the oil industry. The speaking accents of Texans and Oklahomans can be heard on every street corner. Edmonton too is a busy center for airplane traffic. With two airports, it receives planes from all directions, but especially from the great region to the north, where airplanes are an all-important means of transportation.

Such are the prairie provinces — land of grain, of cattle, and of minerals. They contain four-fifths of all the improved farming land in Canada, yet someday they may also produce more than one-half the amount of oil the United States does, and they may be known as much for their mineral as for their agricultural output.

The prairie lands are beef country too. Here a herd of cattle, watched by cowboys, finds water at the South Saskatchewan River. (CANADIAN GOVT. TRAVEL BUREAU PHOTO)

British Columbia has spectacular scenery. A peak in the Rocky Mountains. (BRITISH COLUMBIA GOVT. PHOTO)

British Columbia – Big Country

British Columbia is the most spectacular of the Canadian provinces. It is almost entirely mountainous. From the Rockies in the east to the Coast Mountains in the west the towering peaks climb into the sky. They enclose deep, rich valleys filled with fruit orchards and farms. The lower mountain slopes are covered with some of the largest trees in the world. Nine-tenths of British Columbia is wooded; more than one-third of Canada's cut of timber comes from its mild, damp forests.

Flowers bloom in front of the Legislative Buildings, in Victoria, British Columbia. (NATIONAL FILM BOARD)

British Columbia's climate is influenced by the warm Japan Current that flows along the northwest coast of North America. Warm, moist winds blow inland from the Pacific. The two main cities, Vancouver and Victoria, have hardly any snow. Sports like golf can be played throughout the year. Flowers bloom until Christmas.

Vancouver is Canada's third largest city and second largest port. A magnificent harbor, open throughout the year, serves ships from all over the world, although much of the trade is with the East, out across the Pacific. Like San Francisco to the south, Vancouver has a large, busy Chinatown where colorful shops and restaurants offer unusual things, so different from those of native Canada. It is hard to realize that British Columbia is as close to China as it is to Newfoundland. In the beautiful setting of this fast-growing city Vancouver, swimming, golf, tennis, sailing, and skiing are but minutes away from the heart of downtown. With its temperate climate and its unsurpassed facilities for pleasant living, many people believe that one day Vancouver will be the largest city in the country.

46

British Columbia's other major city, Victoria, is its capital. It lies at the southern tip of Vancouver Island, the largest island on the west coast of the continent. Despite fisheries and lumbering, Victoria is basically a quiet tourist and residential city with flower-lined streets and Canada's gentlest climate. To the north, Vancouver Island becomes mountainous and heavily forested, with one of the largest uninterrupted stands of timber in the world and with rivers where salmon weigh up to eighty pounds.

Vancouver Island meets the ocean in a long series of wooded points. (PHOTO BY HUFFMAN, FROM CUSHING)

The Coastal Mountains of the mainland are cut by many rivers that plunge down to the ocean. Up these rivers in the spring the salmon swim to spawn — lay their eggs — then die. Year after year the cycle is repeated. Probably by sense of smell the salmon find their way back to spawn in the same rivers where they themselves were hatched. In British Columbia, salmon are the most important catch of the fishing industry; they make up two-thirds of its value.

Salmon are taken at the mouths of the rivers by gill net, seine, or troll. A gill net is just what it sounds like. It has floats along its upper edge so that it hangs vertically from the surface of the water, like a curtain across the path of the fish. As they swim into it their heads are caught in the meshes of the net, but their bodies are too large to go through. When they try to withdraw, they are caught by their gills.

A seine is a net with floats, too. It is paid out to encircle a school of fish. As the fish enter the circle the net is pursed, or gathered up, under them. The crew of the fishing boat then scoops them up out of the net, using net baskets called trailers.

These fishing boats are gill netting for salmon in the Fraser River of British Columbia. (BRITISH COLUMBIA GOVT. PHOTO)

A troll is a long line baited with hooks. It is dragged behind a slow-moving boat.

Most of the salmon catch is canned or frozen. The heads and tails are cut off to be made into fertilizer; no part of the fish is wasted.

In large part, British Columbia lies in Canada's unbroken belt of forest, six hundred to one thousand miles wide, which stretches between the Atlantic and the Pacific oceans. In the East, logging is done mainly in the winter. The logs are dragged out of the frozen, snow-filled woods and are often left on river ice to float downstream when spring comes and the ice melts. In British Columbia, lumbering is a year-round business. It is highly mechanized, with huge diesel trucks that haul the logs over roads that are passable all through the year because of the climate.

The felling of the colossal Douglas firs is a highly skilled job. When a tree has been selected — and it may be a tree that is three hundred feet high and as wide across as a small house — the lumberjacks notch the trunk on the side where they want it to fall. They

Two lumbermen saw a felled Douglas fir into manageable lengths in the North Pacific forest. (BRITISH COLUMBIA GOVT. PHOTO)

Logs are often formed into booms and are then towed to sawmills by tugs. (PHOTO BY HUFFMAN, FROM CUSHING)

plan so that it will not damage other trees as it thunders down. When the notch has been axed, the opposite side of the trunk is sawed until the tree topples over the notch and crashes to the ground. The branches are then removed, and the tree is sawed into manageable lengths. Tractors haul the lengths out of the forest to trucks, which carry them to the mills.

Where logs can be easily floated they may be dumped into the rivers. When they have drifted downstream into wide water they are gathered into a sort of huge raft called a boom. They are put into position by boom men, who use long pike poles and short peaveys, or cant hooks, to move them around. These men must be

50

The people of Canada work to preserve their forest areas. Cathedral Grove, in MacMillan Park, on Vancouver Island. (BRITISH COLUMBIA GOVT. PHOTO)

skillful and agile to avoid falling between the logs, where they would instantly be crushed to death.

Although the method makes more hauling necessary, trees selected to be felled may grow very far apart. The reason is that a forest that is being logged over must not be left wholly bare. In bare areas natural reseeding from growing trees cannot take place. The Canadians know the many benefits that come from a forest and they do not wish to destroy them. In modern practices of conservation a stand of forest is cut in such a way that carefully spaced-out trees are left to provide new seeds for the areas that have been cut out. Further, after an area has been cut, natural seeding is

51

helped out by the planting of tiny seedlings that have been grown in tree nurseries especially for this purpose. The government and the forest-industry companies are making sure that the country's wooded areas will add to Canada's well-being over the years to come.

The tourist industry is of great value to British Columbia. The province's beautiful coastal islands, its deep forests, its mountains and river valleys, its winter sports, and its beaches all attract many thousands of visitors. Perhaps the finest hunting country in North America lies back from the settled areas. This country abounds with game — big game like elk, moose, caribou, mountain goat, big-horn sheep, and the vicious grizzly bear. For the less ambitious sportsmen there are duck, goose, quail, trout, and of course, salmon.

Parts of the interior of this big country are so wild and unknown that some people believe a race of primitive men lives there. De--scriptions of members of this race resemble what in India and Tibet is called the Abominable Snowman. Here he is known as the Sas-quatch. Over the years the Sasquatch has been reported always as being entirely covered with hair, and occasionally reaching a height of nine feet. Ordinarily he is supposed to be timid and retiring, but there have been stories of his attacking men or coming close to their dwellings or wilderness camps. Reports of these creatures have come from all over the world, and it may not be impossible that the mountain fastnesses of British Columbia could provide a home for them. At any rate, in 1884 there was a newspaper account of a Sas-quatch who had been injured in a fall and had been captured by several railway workers in the Fraser River Valley. He was nick-named Jacko, and lived in captivity for some time. But there is no report of what happened to him eventually. The mystery remains to this day.

The Mackenzie River Delta, far north, at Aklavik (in the center of the picture). This is desolate and watery country. (PHOTO BY HUNTER, NA-TIONAL FILM BOARD)

High North – The Last Frontier

There are startling contrasts in the nearly unsettled northern areas that make up four-fifths of Canada. From the lofty peaks of the Saint Elias Range in the Yukon, across the flat, treeless plains called tundra, this unbelievable land reaches over desolate islands and the frozen Arctic Ocean toward the North Pole. Here, in the true north, the vastness of Canada can most easily be seen. Here is the continent's second longest river, the Mackenzie—more than twenty-five hundred miles in length. Here are islands a thousand miles

53

long. The last of the Ice Age can be seen in the glaciers on these islands. One, Ellesmere Island, is half covered with ice even in the middle of summer.

What is the Arctic? Probably the best way to describe it is by climate, by the fact that trees do not grow because they generally cannot — the average temperature of the warmest month does not rise above fifty degrees Fahrenheit.

Canada's North, however, is not all Arctic. There is a subarctic region that comes down through the heavily forested areas of the Canadian Shield to within sight of the government buildings in Ottawa and the top of Mount Royal in the middle of Montreal. The wilderness is never far from any Canadian home.

The North came to be known to Europeans through their search for a northwest passage. But it was gold that brought the North from a period of exploration to one of development. In 1896, George Carmack, a prospector, along with two Indians, Tagish Charlie and Skookum Joe, found the gold strike they had been looking for. It was on Bonanza Creek, which flows into the Yukon River. In the eight years that followed, more than one hundred million dollars' worth of gold came out of the region, which is famous as the Klondike.

Miles Canyon, on the Yukon River, about six miles from Whitehorse.
(CANADIAN GOVT. TRAVEL BUREAU PHOTO)

The rush to the West had begun with the discovery of gold in California in 1848. Nine years later, British Columbia's Fraser Valley was struck as the restless miners pushed northward, searching each river valley in the dream of making a fortune overnight. Twenty-five thousand people moved into the area. Within three years the Cariboo Lake country had produced millions of dollars' worth of gold. In one stretch of ground along Williams Creek there were four thousand miners in seven miles. One claim gave up two thousand dollars a day for a whole year.

The Klondike gold rush, however, has never been equaled. More than thirty thousand people struggled and fought their way across the mountains from the Alaskan coast, through Chilkoot Pass, into the interior of the country. One man, who somehow managed to get a cow across into newly founded Dawson City, set up a business of selling milk at ten dollars a quart. Although only a few miners struck it rich, the rush opened up the Yukon. Boats appeared on the rivers, and a railroad was built from Skagway, Alaska, to Whitehorse, in the Yukon. People stayed. Communities developed.

Cape Dorset, in the Northwest Territories, is a settlement among bleak surroundings. (PHOTO BY KORDA, FOR NATIONAL FILM BOARD)

A trapper in the northern forests covers his deadfall trap with evergreen branches. (PHOTO BY SAWDERS, FROM CUSHING)

When other minerals as important as gold were later found, more communities grew up under the watchful eyes of the Mounties. Now silver, copper, zinc, nickel, and oil are important. Just as with any great mining finds, some ores were discovered by chance, some by digging for something else. Canada's fantastic storehouse of mineral treasures was becoming known.

Now, while it certainly is not crowded with people, the North is not empty, either. There are about seventy-five hundred Indians, twelve thousand Eskimos, and more than twenty thousand other persons in the Yukon and the Northwest Territories. These people are everything from tugboat captains to truck drivers, from miners to fishermen, from doctors to nurses and schoolteachers. They work at countless jobs, for the area is no longer primarily hunting and trapping country.

Even the Indians have begun to turn aside from their old wandering way of life. They labor alongside the white settlers in mining or construction or other kinds of work. In winter, though, many Indians still desert the towns for their traplines, and fur is still their largest cash crop. These northern Indians really live in the subarctic, below the tree line, where game is to be found. Unlike the Indians farther south, they exist in small, roving bands; there is not enough game in any one district to support a large tribe. If they wish, however, they may live on a reservation, like many of Canada's other two hundred thousand Indian citizens.

Eskimos are a unique people. They have lived for thousands of years in a land so harsh that Europeans have only recently learned to cope with it. Though the northern Indians live in the forests, most of the Eskimos have never left the barren coastal country. Here they are able to fill their most important needs from the sea. The mainstay of the Eskimos is the seal. It furnishes food, and oil for cooking and for light. Its skin is made into clothing or is cut into long strips to be used like rope. In winter, Eskimos hunt on the ice. In summer they hunt from little skin boats called kayaks and from large ones called umiaks. In summer they also hunt on land for caribou. They use the animal for food, but more especially for its skin, which makes the warmest and lightest of their clothing.

An Eskimo draws a captured seal along the ice in the far north. (PHOTO
BY GRANT, NATIONAL FILM BOARD)

Just as they learned to fill their food and clothing needs from the few animals they could hunt, so also they developed the igloo or snow house in a land where there was almost no building material except snow.

The Eskimos are sociable, hospitable, and cooperative. Above all, they are cheerful. Eskimo children are never punished, but learn to be responsible by carrying out small duties even when they are very young. Everyone in the small, isolated Eskimo communities knows that, if life is to go on, every person must do his part.

This little girl has the cheerful look typical of most of the Eskimo people. (PHOTO BY SPROAT, NATIONAL FILM BOARD)

Now, while the older Eskimos cling to much of their time-honored way of life, the younger people are fitting themselves into a changing world. Many of them have jobs, and work in the modern society that is pressing into the North. They may live in prefabricated houses that have been shipped in from farther south. They may be employed on military installations, or they may be bulldozer drivers, clerks, miners, or mechanics. They are extraordinarily skillful with machinery.

They have set up fishing cooperatives, and handicrafts cooperatives for selling their brilliant carvings and works of art. Within a few years, in an area where just a short time ago there were no schools at all, every Eskimo child will be going to school. Change has been rapid and there can be no turning back. Transportation and communications continue to improve and to reach out over more territory. As they do, they open up, even more, Canada's, and one of the world's, last frontiers.

Canada's Future

As, in 1967, Canada celebrated her one-hundredth birthday as a nation her people may have glanced back, but they looked forward, too. There is still much to be done.

Canada must work to develop her unsettled areas further, though these areas have already made her the world's greatest producer of nickel, asbestos, platinum, and zinc. In gold, uranium, aluminum, cobalt, and wood-pulp production the country is also important to the increasing world demand.

Canada must persuade more of her people to move into the North and settle there. She must build new roads, railroads, and airfields if she is to make the most of the fabulous mineral wealth that is known to exist underground. As yet, the surface of the earth has scarcely been scratched.

In order that the government may best tackle these problems, a new Department of Energy, Mines and Resources has recently been established. It will study ways to develop mining and oil and gas production, and it will decide what should be done about one of Canada's greatest assets — her tremendous supply of water. Should water be exported to drought-stricken areas of the United States? What is the best means of preventing water pollution? These questions and many others will be considered by the new department.

In addition to developing her uninhabited areas and her natural resources further, Canada must somehow settle the very real differences that exist between her two founding nationalities, the French and the English, if she is to move into the future with confidence.

61

She must bring together into her ways of life thousands of immigrants — new Canadians.

She must improve education for her native Indians and Eskimos and teach them new skills so that they may fit into the modern technical society that surrounds them. And her provinces must constantly build new schools and colleges to meet the increasing demands for more highly trained citizens.

As a growing power, Canada must ever play her part in world affairs. Her voice has been heard in such organizations as the United Nations. It must continue to be heard. Only in a world of peace can she continue to develop her riches, her way of life, and her young strength. If she can do that, then, in the words of one of her great prime ministers, Sir Wilfred Laurier, "The twentieth century belongs to Canada."

An old engraving of Marie de L'Incarnation. (PUBLIC ARCHIVES OF CANADA)

Some Famous People in Canada's History

MARIE DE L'INCARNATION

For thirty years this great woman was the Mother Superior of the Ursuline Order of nuns, founded in Quebec in 1639. Her devotion, piety, and self-sacrifice were an inspiration to all around her. The Indians were especially impressed by a faith that would make a woman leave her home to come to a new land to work with and for them. The Ursulines still occupy the site where they had their first building.

This statue by Hébert commemorates the courage of Adam Dollard. (PUBLIC ARCHIVES OF CANADA)

ADAM DOLLARD

All through the early days the Iroquois Indians were determined to wipe out the settlements of New France. In the spring of 1660 two forces totaling eight hundred Iroquois gathered to destroy Montreal. Adam Dollard des Ormeaux, a young French officer, went upriver with sixteen young men and five loyal Indians to intercept one of the Iroquois forces. For one week, with almost certain death facing them, the French group held out against both forces. They caused such terrible losses to the enemy that the Iroquois retired after deciding that if so few men fought so fiercely, a fortified post could not be taken. These brave men saved New France, for without them Quebec and Montreal would have fallen.

MADELEINE DE VERCHERES

In this young girl is another example of the unbelievable courage of the early colonists. Two of her brothers, still in their teens, had been killed by the Iroquois. Her sister had been widowed at thirteen. One day when Madeleine was fourteen and her parents were away, her home was attacked by the Iroquois. For eight days, with the help of two younger brothers and an old man, she held off forty or fifty Indians until a detachment of soldiers from Montreal arrived. In Canada's history her name has come to mean bravery — the bravery without which the colony could not have survived.

ALEXANDER MACKENZIE

As men pushed ever farther west in their search for fur they discovered the rich country around Lake Athabaska in present northern Saskatchewan. Because it was so far from Montreal that the expense of transportation was enormous, the explorers and traders dreamed about waterways leading to the Pacific. In 1789, Alexander Mackenzie set out and paddled down the river that now

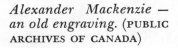

Alexander Mackenzie — an old engraving. (PUBLIC ARCHIVES OF CANADA)

bears his name. He called it River of Disappointment when he realized it flowed into the Arctic. Four years later he headed west down the Peace River. By canoe and on foot he struggled through the Rockies to become the first European, north of Mexico, to journey overland across the continent. At Dean's Channel he was at the ocean. There on a rock he painted:

Alexander Mackenzie from Canada by land
the twenty second of July
one thousand seven hundred and ninety three.

LOUIS RIEL

In two armed rebellions of the West against the Ottawa government the half-breeds were led by Riel. When Canada took over Rupert's Land from the Hudson's Bay Company, the half-breeds had real reason to fear that their land and French language rights would be taken from them. Both rebellions were put down, and Riel was hanged. But his leadership brought the grievances to the attention of the government, and a satisfactory settlement was worked out so that the West came into the dominion without further trouble.

SIR WILFRID LAURIER

Canada's first French Canadian prime minister was a farmer's son. As a child he was sent to live with a Scottish Presbyterian family. Here he gained firsthand knowledge of English Canadians as well as of their language, customs, and religion. Throughout the rest of his life he stood for racial and religious friendship, the rule of law, and for full sharing of French Canadians in the development of Canada as a whole.

SIR FREDERICK BANTING

This distinguished physician, working at the University of Toronto with Charles Best, succeeded in making an extract called insulin. With injections of insulin, patients with the disease called diabetes may lead a normal life. In 1923, Banting became famous all over the world when he received the Nobel prize for his outstanding medical discovery. He lost his life in an airplane crash during World War II.

Sir Wilfrid Laurier.
(PUBLIC ARCHIVES OF CANADA)

Sir Frederick Banting.
(PUBLIC ARCHIVES OF CANADA)

Fortress Louisbourg in process of reconstruction. (NOVA SCOTIA INFORMATION SERVICE PHOTO)

Things to See in Canada

At Louisbourg, on Nova Scotia's Cape Breton Island, are the remains of France's greatest New World fortress. Its capture and destruction in 1758 allowed the British to conquer Quebec and thus all New France. The ruins of the fortress as well as those of the surrounding town are being reconstructed.

Shrine of Ste Anne de Beaupré. (QUEBEC PUBLICITY SERVICE PHOTO)

Three hundred years ago a few Breton sailors, miraculously saved from shipwreck, landed on the shore twenty-one miles below Quebec City. They erected a little chapel to Ste Anne, the patron saint of sailors. The first of a series of marvelous cures of illness took place while the chapel was being built. Now, each year, more than one million people visit the great shrine of Ste Anne de Beaupré, on this same spot.

The reversing falls in the St. John River. (NEW BRUNSWICK TRAVEL BUREAU PHOTO)

The world's highest tides, in the Bay of Fundy between New Brunswick and Nova Scotia, create a reversing waterfall. On the outgoing tide the St. John River in New Brunswick rushes down over fall-like rapids at its mouth. With the incoming tide the river water backs up so that it flows upstream over the same rapids, which then churn and cascade in the opposite direction. In the Petitcodiac River the same tides cause a remarkable wall of water, called a bore, from three to six feet high to rush up the nearly empty river on the incoming tide.

World-famous Niagara Falls, divided by Goat Island, belongs to both Canada and the United States. The Canadian side is called Horseshoe Falls because of its deep curve. At night the falls are lighted by bright searchlights.

The Columbia Ice Fields are in Jasper National Park in Alberta. This huge sea of lasting ice and snow is the largest in the Rocky Mountains and is more than one hundred square miles in area. It is called the "Mother of Rivers," for from its melting glaciers rivers flow into three oceans. The Fraser and Columbia rivers flow west into the Pacific, the Athabaska flows north to the Arctic, and the Saskatchewan flows east to Hudson Bay and the Atlantic.

Lower Fort Garry, near Winnipeg, Manitoba, was built by the Hudson's Bay Company in 1830. It is the only stone fort of the early fur-trading days that has remained unruined. A national park has been created to preserve this reminder of the settling of the West.

Air view of Lower Fort Garry, near Winnipeg, Manitoba. (MANITOBA DEPT. OF INDUSTRY AND COMMERCE PHOTO)

In Thunderbird Park, Victoria, British Columbia, is a collection of remarkable totem poles. Making totem poles was a particular art of the Indian tribes of the American Northwest. The poles are somewhat like coats of arms; the figures carved on them represent objects or animals to which a family group was believed to have blood relationship.

Totem poles at the entrance to Thunderbird Park, in Victoria, British Columbia. (NATIONAL FILM BOARD)

Martyr's shrine at Midland. Ontario. (ONTARIO DEPT. OF TRAVEL & PUBLICITY PHOTO)

The Martyr's Shrine at Midland, Ontario, is a great stone church built as a lasting memorial to eight Jesuit priests who were murdered by Indians as they carried out their missionary duties. Nearby is the mission of Fort Ste Marie, rebuilt exactly as it was in 1649 before it was put to the torch at the time of the destruction of the Huron Nation by the Iroquois.

The rebuilt mission of Fort Ste Marie. (ONTARIO DEPT. OF TOURISM & INFORMATION PHOTO)

There are more than forty national parks in Canada. They range in size from less than an acre to thousands of square miles. Many, like Nova Scotia's Port Royal where Champlain's habitation of 1604 has been faithfully reconstructed, are of historical interest. Others have been selected for scenic and recreational reasons and provide everything from swimming to mountain climbing. From a small beginning less than one hundred years ago, parks in every province have now grown to more than thirty thousand square miles, devoted to the pleasures of Canadians and foreign travelers alike. Any or all of them are well worth visiting.

The oldest building in Canada is just outside Quebec in the town of Sillery. It was built by the Jesuits in 1637. It is preserved today as a museum.

74

Canadian coat of arms.
(NATIONAL FILM BOARD)

Did You Know That—

Canada is an Iroquois word meaning "village." Probably it was one of the first words heard by Jacques Cartier in his encounters with the Indians in 1534.

Canada's emblem is a sprig of maple. The sprig appears at the bottom of the arms of Canada, while at the top is a lion. In its right paw the lion holds a red maple leaf. The maple-leaf sprig also appears on the arms of Ontario and Quebec.

The patriotic anthem "O Canada" was first played in Quebec in 1880. It was composed by Calixa Lavallée with French words by Sir Adolphe Basile Routhier and English words by R. Stanley Weir.

The longest unfortified border in the world runs for 3,986 miles between Canada and its friendly neighbor the United States.

Asbestos may have been discovered by a little boy. Fibers that he had pulled out of the soil were knitted by his mother into a pair of socks. When they were left by mistake on a hot stove they did not burn. The story is that from this accident Canada's asbestos-mining industry had its start. Today Canada is the world's leading producer of asbestos.

Canada has the largest known oil reserves in the world in the bituminous sands at McMurray, Alberta.

Ontario operated the first aerial forest-fire service in the world, and Saskatchewan had the first aerial ambulance service.

The largest herd of bison left from the vast hordes that used to roam the West is in Wood Buffalo National Park. Here, on the border between Alberta and the Northwest Territories, fifteen thousand animals live protected by the government.

North of Mexico, Quebec City is the only walled city in North America.

More freight tonnage passes through the locks at Sault Ste Marie (Ontario and Michigan) than through the Panama and Suez canals together, despite the eight-month season. (The locks are closed by ice in winter.)

The twin cities of Port Arthur and Fort William, at the head of Lake Superior, make up the largest wheat depot in the world. They have storage facilities for ninety-three million tons.

The Reverend Josiah Henson, the Uncle Tom of Harriet Beecher Stowe's world-famous book, *Uncle Tom's Cabin,* escaped to Canada in 1830 and settled in the village of Dresden, Ontario. There, for many years, he looked after refugee slaves who made their way north by means of the so-called Underground Railway, an escape route maintained by people who were against slavery.

Index